A

Charlotte Mason Education

Catherine Levison

HomeWord-Bound Publications

A Charlotte Mason Education, A How-To Manual

© 1996 by Catherine Levison

ISBN 0-9655044-0-9
Library of Congress Catalog Card Number 96-228741

Levison, Catherine
        A Charlotte Mason Education; A How-To Manual /
        Catherine Levison

Published by: Charlotte Mason Communiqué-tions
                4441 South Meridian, Suite 221
                Puyallup, WA 98373

First Printing, 1996
Second Printing, 1997
Third Printing, 1997
Fourth Printing, 1998
Fifth Printing, 1998

To obtain additional copies or schedule a speaking engagement with the author please write,

Charlotte Mason Communiqué-tions
4441 South Meridian, Suite 221
Puyallup, WA 98373

TABLE OF CONTENTS

ACKNOWLEDGMENTS

I would like to thank Deborah O'Brien for all her help in editing this book; she was more than generous with her time and a very supportive friend during the entire process.

I would also like to thank Victoria Waters, whose generosity with her research and materials has enriched my understanding of Charlotte Mason's philosophy.

Finally, I thank my family, particularly my oldest daughter, for all of their help and support.

INTRODUCTION

It is not the intention of this book to replace any previously written work. In fact, there is no substitute for reading Charlotte Mason's six-volume set entitled *The Original Home Schooling Series.* You may obtain these from libraries, or they may be purchased from several home school catalogs and retail outlets. You may wish to donate a set to your home school support group or share a set with some close friends. Also, Susan Schaeffer Macaulay has written *For the Children's Sake,* which condenses Charlotte's philosophies into a very readable summary of the six-volume set. It was this book that led Dean and Karen Andreola to start the Charlotte Mason Research and Supply Company and reprint the six-volume set. We also owe Karen Andreola our appreciation for the production of the *Parents' Review.* This newsletter is helpful and enjoyable, and the back issues, which are frequently referred to throughout this book, are available by writing to P. O. Box 936, Elkton, MD 21922-0936.

I am pleased to point out the Charlotte Mason method does not involve the purchasing of a curriculum and once understood could be done solely through the library at no cost. However, there are a number of catalog companies that offer many of the materials that Charlotte Mason families enjoy having on hand. Lifetime Books &

Gifts is one of these. They may be reached by writing to 3900 Chalet Suzanne Drive, Lake Wales, FL 33853-7763 or call 1-800-377-0390. Another popular catalog company is The Elijah Company at 1053 Eldridge Loop, Crossville, TN 38558 or call 1-888-235-4524. And one other is Great Christian Books at 229 So. Bridge St., P. O. Box 8000, Elkton, MD 21922-8000 or call 1-800-775-5422.

One very important thing I always stress to people is to pray about your home schooling choices, your book selections, and your children's futures. I strongly recommend you find a trusted prayer partner and promise to pray for each other's school **every day**.

With prayer and thought you can avoid over buying. With very few exceptions, one thing you might want to keep in mind is **you can always make another order**. Most products available for educating children are still going to be available later in the year. Also, just because a book is mentioned by Charlotte Mason, or any advocate of her method, or me, does not make it necessarily appropriate for your family. This method is not hinging on a certain selection of books; on the contrary, this style can be applied to any set of books. You can be as discriminating as you want to be and still use the C. M. method. I happen to be a very particular mother when it comes to reading material. I'll give you one personal example of my convictions. I destroyed our set of the *Chronicles of Narnia* a long time ago, and I have no regrets. Many people love those books, and that is fine by me. We can all give each other a little elbow room to make these choices. On the other hand, I previously rejected all Charles Dickens because of *A Christmas Carol.* I did not allow any ghost stories in my house. I now know I was missing out on *David Copperfield* and *Oliver Twist*, which are two of the best written and most touching fictional books I have ever read. So I have learned to censor out a chapter of a book rather than discarding the whole book. We can take what is good and godly from literature, praying about each choice according to our own convictions.

The intention of this book is to pull out the "how-to" from the philosophy, which can be difficult. Not so that you will never have to read Charlotte Mason for yourself, but so that you can begin to apply her insights right away. We do not always know precisely what the Charlotte Mason schools and home schools did. The reason for this is that the program was changed term to term to keep it from becoming stagnant. Not that they replaced books each term because many of them took up to three years to read. Changing the program kept it fresh for both the teacher and the student. Also, the records for what the home schools used are reported to be gone.

I eased slowly into the method over many years. I would read an idea and then try it on Friday afternoons after we had finished our textbook/workbook system for the week. I found it extremely fun so I started doing all Charlotte Mason in the summers after we had finished the year's work. I was very compulsive about finishing each book and filling in every workbook blank. At this point we are starting our seventh year of home schooling, and we use the C. M. method full time. I do not expect anyone to make overnight changes, and I am not asking you to. One way to make the transition would be to use your textbooks (if that is your current system) as an outline for the material you will cover that year and augment the material with some living books. On occasion I may continue to use a textbook this way, because I have a large collection of textbooks on hand and don't see any reason to discard them. It also may be wise to instruct a child how to use a textbook, or how to a get an "A" in the event they ever attend a class not conducted in the Charlotte Mason way.

You possibly have noticed a dichotomy within the group that adheres to the Charlotte Mason method. There are structured homes and relaxed homes both following the method. Most in the relaxed group have subscribed to Karen's *Parents' Review*. Karen has a way of putting the reader at ease. I enjoy reading her work as I need to loosen up from a compulsive background. Others have never read the current *P. R.* and have been reading Charlotte Mason's books. These families have formed a more structured interpretation because the structure comes through when one reads how C. M.'s students did things. Both styles are valid, and I hope we home schoolers will allow one another the choice.

It has occurred to me that educating our children could be likened to a cross-country automobile ride. We see new things every day. We can learn and experience diverse countryside and people. In other words it can be **fun**. My home schooling is fun and I want yours to be as well. However, like a long road trip, sometimes there will be monotonous stretches (or areas we need to study) but remember there is so much to see and do—one day deserts, the next mountains and waterfalls.

Please do not take offense as I offer a further analogy. Some of you are in the fast lane, **way** over the speed limit. You're racing past the beauty and maybe even heading for a collision (with perhaps burnout?). Others of you have been in the rest area **way too long**. Please try. Please get back into the car; you can take the slow lane and enjoy yourself. Remember there are plenty of rest areas up ahead. You can pull over as often as needed. Please forgive me, you in the third group, but your car is in the garage. I'm sure you have your reasons, but try to surmount them. Take little baby steps out there, buckle your children's seat belts, and with God's help back out of your driveway. You can have well-educated children and broaden your own horizons too.

CHARLOTTE MASON

Charlotte was born in England in 1842 and was primarily educated by her parents at home. She became orphaned at the age of sixteen. She decided at a young age to make education her life's work and held many positions. She wrote geography books that were popular and then wrote *Home Education*. This book was well received, and she personally corresponded with many of the readers. Their inquiries of how to obtain a teacher for their children who understood these methods caused Charlotte to establish a training college for governesses. At this time the Parents National Education Union (PNEU) was established. She had day schools in England and home schools that were conducted correspondence style, thus the reference to her being called the "founder of the home schooling movement." England at that time was not much different from the present day United States regarding the schools parents had to choose from. They had boarding schools, private day schools, and public schools (since compulsory education had been established in 1880). They also had governesses. It appears many parents did not want their children in the public schools and many could not afford private education, so they home educated. Charlotte Mason began a monthly magazine called the *Parents' Review*, and its purpose was to support the parents of her schools. The magazine continued until the 1960's even though Charlotte passed away in 1923. Copies of this magazine are in the Library of Congress in the United States; Great Britain also has copies, which they made available to Karen Andreola, who is the editor of the current *Parents' Review*. To learn about Charlotte Mason's life, read *The Story of Charlotte Mason* by Essex Cholmondeley, which, although out of print, may be obtained through interlibrary loan in the United States.

Charlotte was very much admired by so many people who have left us with their accounts of having known her. She was a devoted Christian woman who loved children. She wrote in 1862, "Truly parents are happy people—to have God's children lent to them...I love my children dearly."

THE METHOD IN BRIEF

Charlotte Mason covers a lot of topics. Since I do not want to replace her writings, I am choosing the most essential topics so you have a starting place. She advocates a liberal (generous) education. She likens it to the old saying of leading a horse to water and asks us if we are even leading the children to the water. She believes children are born persons and that all children should be educated by the humanities. She wants them to have a love for learning and for us not to kill that love.

We are leading them to self education. This is done through direct contact with the best books, and the adult stays out of the way in the sense of not lecturing. We rely heavily on narration instead of comprehension questions or workbooks to verify knowledge. Examinations are done with a view to see what the child does know, not to expose what they don't know. Charlotte Mason students learn a body of information and are told to tell all they know about President Lincoln, or leaves, or the Atlantic Ocean. This is essay style. Currently in the United States, our inclination is to teach a body of information and then test to see what they did not catch.

There is an emphasis on whole books and living books. A whole book is what the author wrote. The child is allowed to read the entire book (hopefully well chosen) of a great author. How else would you ever have had contact with these gifted authors? The opposite of a whole book is an anthology or a reader comprised of selections of different writers' works. A living book is the opposite of a textbook. Not that textbooks or encyclopedias are bad. Many people like them; they are useful at times and have probably improved since Charlotte's day. But they contain facts. Just facts. Living books have lives, emotion, people are married, and pass away. They are usually what Charlotte calls "clothed in literary language." An accurate historical novel or a biography is a good example.

The system consists of short morning lessons with a large variety of subjects. Charlotte says it is the hours the children spend working, not the quantity of subjects, that fatigues them. Their minds are invigorated by switching subjects as diverse as possible at fifteen-minute increments. Focused and full attention is paid to between fifteen and twenty-one subjects depending on their age. (See Appendix—not all subjects are covered every day.) They have all afternoon and evening free to enjoy being a child, to pursue hobbies, and to read. They are not assigned homework but most home schools do not anyway. They are not allowed to dawdle during lessons. At our house we get the book we will need and set the timer. This really works; my children thrive under this format.

Smooth parenting is based on the formation of good habits so I have included a brief section on that topic at the end of the book.

The children's motto is "I am, I can, I ought, I will." Charlotte chose this in 1891. She says every child can say "I am" because they are a child of God, a gift to their parents. "I can" stands for having the power God has given us to do a thing. "I ought" has to do with duty. "I will" is different from I want. It is the child's decision to do what is right.

The motto for the parents and/or educators is "Education is an atmosphere, a discipline, a life." There is much written about this, but as a start I suggest just mulling over what it says and asking yourself if your home is like this. In a 1935 *Parents' Review* article reprinted in the current *P. R.* Volume 2 (Summer 1992) on the topic of the children's motto, E. Kitching says, "We have a definite mission—to bring fullness of life to the children. It is more possible to carry this mission in a home schoolroom."

NARRATION

Narration is assimilating information and retelling it. Anyone would listen closely if they knew they were going to retell what they had heard. Just like when you've seen a documentary and tell your friend all about it the next day, you will remember it better.

Charlotte Mason uses an illustration of a doctor visiting a sick person in the hospital. The patient is in extreme pain and the doctor has written the remedy on a three-by-five card. He tells her this will alleviate the pain, however, he's only going to let her look at the card for a few minutes. Then the card will be destroyed permanently, and he won't be writing it for her ever again. Can you imagine the attention you would give to that card? This is the kind of attention Charlotte wants the children to pay to their reading. When they are retelling they have to leave some information out and that's one of the choices being made by their minds. Charlotte says it is not a mere act of memory because we let their minds act on the material in their own original way. They will classify and connect information. Remember, you **cannot narrate what you do not know. If you can narrate it, you know it.**

Narration can be used in all school subjects and in all experiences. Charlotte says years later the child will be able to narrate the same passage with "vividness, detail and accuracy of the first telling."

HOW TO: You read aloud to them one single reading, only about 10 to 13 minutes for each book. This is very important to have their full attention. Don't stop to define words during the reading; they'll usually understand the sentence or paragraph anyway. Ask one of the listeners to tell you what you just read. If they hesitate, ask them if they remember one thing of what you read. If they seem reluctant and I know they understood, I'll usually make a joke like, "Oh, I see, well I guess it was about a pink rabbit who met an elephant?" This always makes them laugh since this probably was not what Robin Hood or Gideon was just doing in our story and they start telling you what it was about. Only let one child narrate per reading. You don't correct them, but if another child points out an error that's okay. Charlotte says to not interrupt a narration. Most kids narrate easily because we tend to do this as people—we relive events (or books) with others. Your child has probably told you all about some event he witnessed or every detail of a show he saw. This is the same thing. It's casual and natural, which is why it differs from a book report. So, don't make more of it than it is.

Narration is a very powerful learning tool. Charlotte Mason tells us (and she's right) that perfect attention and absolute recollection is an asset to employer, teacher, and the nation. She says adults read and forget but her students "have the powers of perfect recollection and just application because they have read with attention and concentration and have in every case reproduced what they read in narration." She also points out that many professions wish they could grasp the content on a single reading. For some children it takes a little more practice. One child, whose test results showed he was behind one full grade level in "listening" on the IOWA Basic Skills test, is now narrating with a "photographic memory."

They begin narration at six years old, and they do it orally. They tell, you listen. You may take dictation if you care to and file those as often as you desire. Don't let it become a burden to you though. To prevent that I often take down the narration at the end of the book with only an occasional chapter narration. Most books take us three to four months to read. If I wrote out each oral narration they ever told me, I would not be doing much else. I know one mom who uses a tape recorder as a time saver and a way to not have to stop or slow down the child while she takes dictation. This could be useful with many children, but I would take the time to listen to them narrate in person as often as I could.

At ten years old they begin to write out their narrations. This can be a long process. Give them all the time they need (I mean a year if needed) to make this transition. The Hon. Mrs. E. L. Franklin wants us to be cautious not to begin too early with written narration or nature notebooks. Accept their written work without undue concern for the punctuation, capitalization, or the spelling. These "skills" will improve with practice and with the reading the child will be doing. I will, on occasion, point out in a lighthearted way one very important error such as the pronoun "I" not being capitalized. Keep in mind these narrations are not done for the purpose of spotting errors.

You see, the young child is being read to before he can read. They can be learning the Bible, history, and geography before they are six years old. Charlotte says a child of six has begun his education; it doesn't matter whether he understands each and every word. It matters that he learn to deal directly with books. That's why what you choose to read to them is so important. Charlotte Mason wants them exposed to the best in literature, poetry, music, and art. She most definitely does not want them in what we call "dumbed-down" books. She calls literature written down to the child's level "twaddle."

LITERATURE

Education "classroom style" developed in Europe and America without the funds for books. Teachers had to take their knowledge and convey it through lecturing. This began the use of the blackboard as well. In a 1923 publication called *In Memoriam of Charlotte M. Mason*, H. W. Household says the teacher "must be able to hold attention; to make a large class move as one individual; to push all through a ridiculous and soul-destroying examination on the result of which his meager pay depended. He must be a disciplinarian, with an air of command, and a strong right arm." (I say, if you take out the discipline and the strong right arm, you have today's schools and maybe that's the whole problem!)

Charlotte thought a child is "in danger of receiving much teaching with little knowledge," and she thought a book-less education was a contradiction in terms. Thus her predominant theme of **don't get between the child and the book, don't talk too much, and don't lecture.** Even if the school had books, Charlotte thought school books were **dry**. She said the teachers knew this too and that is also why they lectured. Since Charlotte thinks lectures are a waste of time and strain on the children's attention, she wanted them in the right books with a single reading. Her opinion is that the mind will put off the effort of attention as long as a second or third chance exists of getting the information. She says "complete and entire attention is a natural function which requires no effort and causes no fatigue."

Since the children will be concentrating so intensely on their reading material, we had better choose wisely, with much discernment; at the same time we want to lead them to the greater "classic" works. Our goal is to develop good literary taste in our homes. The currently written "literature" available at book stores has been written at the average eighth-grade reading level. Charlotte's students were exposed to Plutarch, Shakespeare, Dickens, and great poets before they were in eighth grade. Charlotte said the child must enjoy the book, and she felt life was too short to be spent in books that are dull. "The ideas it holds must each make that sudden, delightful impact upon their minds, must cause that intellectual stir," she tells us. She recommends *Swiss Family Robinson* as better for the child's imagination than *Alice in Wonderland*. Charlotte did not go for short goody-goody books. When our children read books like the Bible, *Little Women,* or *David Copperfield*, they will make evaluations on the morals and distinguish between good and evil decisions being made and the consequences of living by them.

As to the question of whether we read to them or whether they read the books for themselves, both are done. They need to **see** words, paragraphs, well-constructed sentences, and punctuation. If a book is over their reading ability we read it to them so they can benefit from its contents. The Hon. Mrs. E. L. Franklin is quoted to say, "We shall not lightly abandon this custom of reading aloud to children, even when they are grown boys and girls."

In PNEU schools the literature they chose augmented the period of history they were studying. Following is a list of books they used. Please use your own judgment and discernment. (This list does not necessarily reflect my personal preferences—please see Introduction.)

SIX TO NINE YEARS OLD

Andersen's Fairy Tales   *Grimm's Fairy Tales*
David Copperfield—Dickens   *Just So Stories*—Kipling
Pilgrim's Progress—Bunyan   *Water Babies*—Kingsley
Alice in Wonderland—Carroll   *Aesop's Fables*
Tales From Shakespeare—The Lambs
Mrs. Gatty's—*Parables from Nature*
Tales of Troy and Greece—Andrew Lang

SEVEN TO EIGHT YEARS OLD

Tanglewood Tales—Hawthorne
Robinson Crusoe—DaFoe

NINE TO ELEVEN YEARS OLD

Shakespeare's *Twelfth Night*   Walter Scott's *Rob Roy*
Gulliver's Travels—Swift   *Kidnapped*—Stevenson
The Heroes of Asgard—Keary   Charles Dickens

TWELVE TO FOURTEEN YEARS OLD

History of English Literature   Shakespeare's Histories
Poetry

FIFTEEN TO EIGHTEEN YEARS OLD

Essay on Man—Pope   *Essay on Burns*—Carleyle
The Virginians—Thackeray
Jessamy Bride—Frankfort Moore
Citizen of the World—Goldsmith

SEVENTEEN TO EIGHTEEN YEARS OLD

Poetry
She stoops to Conquer (a play)
Essays on Goldsmith—Macaulay
The Battle of the Books—Boswelel

Some of these books may be out of print but can be obtained through interlibrary loans or at used book stores. I've found looking at book stores near universities to be best for locating these kinds of titles. The more you know about the book the easier for the librarian to do a nation-wide search. On Mrs. Gatty's for example, her full name is either Mrs. Alfred Gatty or Margaret Scott Gatty. Her life span was 1809 to 1879. The 1914 edition is at the University of Montana and at Whitman College in Washington. The 1976 edition is at Washington State University and Anchorage (Alaska) Library.

MY BOOK LIST

Aesop's Fables	*Anne of Green Gables*
Anne of Avonlea	*Heidi*
At the Back of the North Wind	*The Call of the Wild*
Black Beauty	*Great Dog Stories*
Kidnapped	*Treasure Island*
Little Men	*Little Women*
The Prince and the Pauper	*Pollyanna*
Rebecca of Sunnybrook Farm	*Robin Hood*
The Swiss Family Robinson	*Robinson Crusoe*

Tales from Shakespeare
A Little Princess (excluded 15th chpt)
The Legend of Pocahontas (excluded 2nd chpt)
The Secret Garden (excluded 23rd chpt)

All of the above are published by Children's Classics and are available at retail stores and Great Christian Books.

Little House series	*Eight Cousins*
Walden	*A Gathering of Days*
Key to the Prison	*Treasures of the Snow*
The House at Pooh Corner	*Jo's Boys*
Winnie-the-Pooh	*Shakespeare*
Howard's End	*A Room with a View*
Silas Marner	*The Lifted Veil*
Brother Jacob	*Middlemarch*
The Portrait of a Lady	*The Turn of the Screw*
The Custom of the Country	*Dr. Zhivago*
Sense and Sensibility	*Oliver Twist*
Emma	*David Copperfield*
Persuasion	*Bleak House*
Pride and Prejudice	*A Tale of Two Cities*
Quite Early One Morning	*Jane Eyre*

The Caine Mutiny   *Wuthering Heights*
The Scarlet Letter   *Twice Told Tales*
The House of Seven Gables
Where Angels Fear to Tread
Hans Brinker or the Silver Skates
Children's Stories From Dickens—Mary Dickens

These are the books I keep at home so I don't have to go to the library, place holds, and wait. I have found some of these novels to be too long to enjoy under the pressure of a three- to six-week return date. This is not an exhaustive list of classics. I have been investing in hard-bound books with acid-free paper; however, some I've collected in paperback. Again, you can use your library and read all these free. You can also watch garage sales and used book outlets—just make sure they are the **unabridged** version. A helpful book for making book selections is *Let the Authors Speak* by Carolyn Hatcher. She has Charlotte Mason-type books arranged in lists. One list is by century and location, another is by title, and the third is by author. To order write to Old Pinnacle Publishing, Dept. 100, 1048 Old Pinnacle Rd, Joelton, TN 37080.

POETRY

When Monk Gibbon addressed a group of educators in London in 1936 on the subject of poetry, he stressed the need to enjoy it. This priority will take you past studying, criticizing, dissecting, comparing, and analyzing. Do not think of poetry as a school subject or a curriculum. When Mr. Gibbon saw children, he wanted them to "grow up to be good athletes and they should be lovers of poetry." This sounded very novel to me, as I was raised in the day of being either a gifted athlete or a bookworm. You may read the entire address by back-ordering Volume 2 (Winter 1992/1993) of the current *Parents' Review*. A few highlights from that address would be that you can't make any child like a poem against their will. If you like poetry or a particular poem, it will show. Make sure not to push or "praise too much beforehand." Generally if one likes a poem they do not tend to talk a lot about it anyway. If you don't like poetry, just leave the child and poem alone together.

HOW TO: Charlotte Mason wants us to choose good poetry suited to their age. Select simple poems within the child's own range of imagination but remember to choose noble not twaddle. The Hon. Mrs. E. L. Franklin suggests we choose the best children's poems as well as hymns and Psalms to memorize. When the child is

six years old read to them a poem such as *Wynken,
Blynken, and Nod*. This reading would be done while
they're doing something else, at odd times. This is a sharp
contrast to the total attention paid for the purposes of
narration. Charlotte says they will be able to memorize
and recite the poem from hearing it in this casual way. Do
not make it weary for them. Obviously as they age the
selections will be more mature and longer. Mr. Gibbon
suggests they memorize short Shakespearean passages.
You may also wish to back-order Volume 4 (Winter 1994)
of the current *Parents' Review* to read Karen Andreola's
short article on how her family includes poetry.

At our house I have the child select a poem, and I
post it on the wall next to where they eat. They see it
often enough that way. I still do this even if they can't
read yet because it reminds me of what poem they are
working on. We get poetry books from the library and if
we **really** like the poet then we buy the book, locating it
by providing the ISBN number to the book store.
Sometimes we find out that even a famous poet is not as
pleasing to our family as they may be to another. We use
Favorite Poems Old and New, selected by Helen Ferris,
who has indexed the poems by author, title, and first
lines. The poems are grouped into topics such as pets.
This book is available at most book stores. We also use
The Book of 1000 Poems as recommended by the
Andreolas. These poems are also arranged for easy use,
and it has good indexes, including a subject index. You
may purchase this one from Great Christian Books (see
Introduction). These types of anthologies are good to have

on hand so you don't always have to run to the library. There may be poems you find objectionable in any book, so I suggest you censor out poem by poem rather than discarding an entire poet.

COMPOSITION

Charlotte Mason advises us to not wear ourselves out teaching or drilling young children in composition. She assures us they will be able to write if they have had good books. There is a strong warning in *Home Education* not to hamper the child with instruction, and she prints an example of what **not** to do on pages 245–246. Charlotte reminds us in this same section of our job to "provide children with material in their lessons, and, leave the handling of such material to themselves." (p. 247)

The young children between six and nine years old are not responsible for written narrations (compositions) yet. Charlotte's students in that age group would be asked to tell all they knew about feeding the four thousand, building the tabernacle, various historical events, or how we know the world is round.

Children who are ten to eleven years old have begun written narrations. They will learn punctuation and capitalization by seeing so much well-written literature. Composition will come naturally to children who have spent time with books. They have learned through oral narration that writing is really talking with some rules. When they are nine to twelve years old they can write essays or tell orally from their history, Bible,

Shakespeare, Goldsmith's or Wordworth's poetry as Charlotte suggests. This is how composition becomes a part of all other school subjects and is not really considered a separate subject.

During the junior high years (7th to 9th grade), you may ask them to write on subjects they are really interested in. Do not prohibit writing at any age. Examples of her students' work are printed in *A Philosophy of Education* (Vol. 6, pgs. 195–209).

When the children are in high school (10th to 12th grade), composition becomes a subject to be taught. Even then we are not to "teach" much. In 10th grade have them take notes on history, literature, and their art study. Let them write letters to the editor of a newspaper. During 11th and 12th grade have them write essays on current events. They can also write poems. I have my high school student write research papers, which she does enjoy doing. She also uses her free time to write friendly letters and newsletters.

HANDWRITING

Keeping the short lessons in mind, try Charlotte's advice on accomplishing something perfectly. She would rather see a few perfect A's or B's than a whole page full of sloppy A's. When you think about it, she's right. Can't you picture your child's handwriting sheet? At first they look good, but by the end of the page the letters are smaller, slanting, and becoming sloppy and rushed-looking. We want them to form good habits, and we do not want them to get into bad habits. This is not so we can make them into neurotic perfectionists. We want them to concentrate for a short amount of time and do their best.

When the children are young they practice the alphabet, beginning with the capital letters before the lower case (pretty standard). However, when they are older their handwriting is done by transcribing (copying). Let them pick their favorite passages from a book, the Bible, or poetry and have them transcribe into a "copy" book. We have been using those composition books that are lined according to grade level. They have been inexpensive for us, but I am going to try those attractive blank books you can find at the book stores. My goal is for them to know I value what they are doing. I also want them to value their own work, so if it's in a quality book and they have their choices neatly transcribed, it should be something they'll want to keep.

SPELLING

According to Charlotte Mason, spelling depends upon a photographic, detailed picture of a word. This is a power and a habit to be cultivated in the child right from the start. Now before I explain how to do this I know there are some of you who, like me, have taught and believe in phonics. Phonics have their place in learning to read but, unfortunately in spelling, English does not always follow the rules. As you attempt to have an open mind on this topic, think of this—how many times in your life have you written out a word to see if it looked right?

HOW TO: If you want to teach how to spell a word the Charlotte Mason way then write it on the white board (I'd suggest in black marker) and let the children look at it. You could substitute with a black board or paper if necessary. The children look at the word and shut their eyes to see if they can still "see" it. If they can't, have them open their eyes, look all they want to, and try again. When they think they have it, erase the word and have them write the word. There will rarely be an error. If there is one, have them erase or use white-out and write the word correctly over the space. This works. We want to prevent false spelling as much as possible by not looking at misspelled words. This is why **dictation**, used without prior preparation, is bad for spelling. I, like many of you, had used a method of dictation which was done for the purpose of exposing what words they did not know how to spell, along with capitalization and punctuation errors. Remember, we don't ever want them to see words spelled wrong if possible.

In order to do dictation correctly, we prepare the passage together. The child of eight to nine years old prepares a paragraph; the older child, one to three pages. Identify all words that either of you think will need some attention. Write those words on the board and use the above process, erasing studied words one by one. Then dictate the passage, erasing or whiting out errors, if any. Study those words again and write them in correctly. To me this was further use of that concept of finding out what they do know instead of looking for what they don't know. Erasing the word physically is a tangible act of what you're attempting to do mentally.

Charlotte says that bad spelling is usually a sign of sparse reading or hasty reading without the habit of seeing the words because the children are skimming over them. A lot of time spent reading over the course of years will help you visualize (spell).

If you want to seek remedial help in this area or just have to have a spelling book on hand, I highly recommend either *The ABC's and All Their Tricks* or *Natural Speller*. Both of these are non-consumable books that group words (e.g., ground, round, and sound) into lists. You could think of these yourself but it is well worth the $18.00 to $24.00 for someone else to do it. These are available through home school curriculum stores and catalogs.

FOREIGN LANGUAGES

Charlotte Mason's students covered several European languages rather thoroughly, and French seemed to be a priority—most likely for its close proximity to England. We in the United States may choose our foreign languages for a variety of other reasons.

HOW TO: The order for learning French was to first learn the words orally. Secondly, they learned to read and write in the language. Lastly, they learned the grammar. Since speaking French was the first goal, the PNEU schools felt they were working with the ear not the eye. Of course they wanted to avoid developing bad habits of poor pronunciation and prevented that by employing French people to teach French to their children. Several families usually shared one French woman, and in the Charlotte Mason schools they had a French woman come to class about three hours a week. One alternative I thought of for this might be using an audio program that could be obtained at the library.

If the children are young when you start (and they are supposed to be young), some tips given in the original *Parents' Review* (April 1892, April 1890, December 1908) and in Charlotte's books include starting with simple words for the objects around the room. They can pick up about six a day. Try to use these words in sentences and keep them in use. Convert their favorite games into French, such as "house" or "tea party." They can play lotto by having pictures of household objects in front of them. The parent reads a list of words (in French), and they turn over the picture as they hear the word. The first to "black out" wins. The children must memorize the French verbs but they learn them in sentence form and not as lists.

When the children are between seven and twelve, they can begin learning to read by having you help them translate a little passage. They re-read it in French and then narrate it. At this age in the PNEU schools a French lady would read to them from a French book, and they would narrate in French. Charlotte's students learned Italian and German the same way. They also learned Latin with the same method only they concentrated far more on a thorough study of grammar, syntax, and style. They caution us to use only the best Latin, however, so the child realizes that Latin is a language and not merely grammar. When the children grew older they added forty French phrases every sixty school days. Between nine to fourteen years old they should speak and understand French and be able to read an easy French book. The same was expected in German only with less progress. At this age they should be reading in Latin. By the time they are fourteen years old they studied the history and literature of France, Germany, and England, equally. Each essay they wrote was done in the corresponding language.

Spelling was taught the same way as in English by writing the word and forming a mental image.

In our home we have studied New Testament Greek by purchasing a transliteration, numerically coded to Strong's dictionary. We have used Zodhiates's *The Complete Word Study New Testament* for easy parsing. We have many other reference books of this nature that I want my children using to become more familiar with the original languages of the Bible. We also use *English From the Roots Up*. We own both the book and the flash cards, but I assure you the benefit is in the flash cards, and you can ignore buying the book. You only need one set of flash cards per family—although the instructions speak of one for each child, they were written for classrooms. We also have enjoyed *Rummy Roots* and recommend this highly. These products do not actually teach Greek or Latin as a language, but they do teach Greek and Latin words and how they correspond with English words.

If you want a fun Latin course try *Ecce Romani* by Longman. They have you reading in Latin the very first lesson and every lesson. I chose a junior high level from a large selection of grade levels, so I could use it for several children. I bought parts 1A and 1B with the activity sheets and teacher guides. The ordering numbers are: 79741 teacher guide, 79728 1A student's book, 79729 1B student's book, 79733 activity workbook, and 79734 activity workbook. Unless your child is going to medical school do **not** buy all that I bought. You will enjoy and learn a lot from only purchasing the student book, 1A. You won't need the answer book (teacher guide) or workbooks. Write or call for more information. Longman, 1 Jacob, Reading, MA 01867, 1-800-266-8855 or 1-800-552-2259.

GRAMMAR

In *Home Education* Charlotte admits that grammar is not an attractive subject and we should not hurry the children into it. She would prefer we wait until the child was about ten years old to begin grammar so that they would have had practice with narration.

I'll give you a tip—she writes off and on in the series about grammar, but don't bother reading it because all of it has been put in one book that Karen Andreola has revised called *Simply Grammar*. I have used this book for years and **every** person I've recommended it to has liked it. The reason it works, I believe, is that it teaches one concept at a time. You take your child and the book and sit on the couch for fifteen or so minutes and do it orally together. I suppose they could write out the exercises if they were older and you did not have the time for that subject. After years of looking at every thing else on the market and becoming frustrated with correcting workbooks that had the child underline this and point an arrow to that and circle the whatever, I am very happy with something so easy. Most importantly though is that it works. This book is available at Great Christian Books and many other home school catalog distributors such as the Timberdoodle Company. They may be reached at 1-800-478-0672 or write to them at E. 1510 Spencer Lake Road, Shelton, WA 98584. If you live in the Northwest it may be purchased retail at any Christian Supply store.

SCIENCE

You may have read *Home Education*, the first volume of Charlotte's series, and would already be aware of her emphasis on taking the younger children outside every day to be in direct contact with nature. She really means every day, and she lived with the less-than-perfect weather of England. The objective is to help the child learn to be observant. The parent can relax, sit on a blanket, bring a project or a book along, and make this a leisurely outing. Casually point out scenery around your children. Charlotte suggests we ask them "who can see the most and tell the most about..." any plants, insects, or anything nearby. This appears to be an early form of narration to me. With as little talking as possible and absolutely no lecturing, attempt to have them notice the geography of the area, the position of the sun, the weather, and the clouds.

Take them to places where they will find things worth observing. Charlotte wanted children to have beautiful memories of their childhood stored for their old age and thought too many of us have blurry memories due to the fact we did not slow down and really look at things. To remedy this, she suggests that on rare occasions we have the child take a mental photograph of some scenic landscape. Have the child look, then shut their eyes and describe the scene. If it is too blurry in their minds, have them open their eyes, look again, and make a second attempt.

Getting outside this often can be difficult, I know. I live with rainy coastal conditions, and I tend to not be an outdoor person. However, there is refreshment and a literal re-creation involved that makes this worth the effort. Living in an urban or suburban area is going to make finding a natural setting more difficult. Our family has done a fair amount of nature observation in our cultivated suburban yard, and one advantage I can think of is that I know the names of the trees we've planted. If planning regular trips out of the city seems impossible to you, start small, and don't be discouraged. Cities always have parks and arboretums. Maybe you can plan a family vacation with a new outlook of getting to more natural places.

We read in *School Education* (Vol. 3) that in "science or rather nature study, we attach great importance to recognition." Some examples are plants, stones, constellations, birds, field crops, and leaves. On the other hand the PNEU schools say they were "extremely careful not to burden the verbal memory with scientific nomenclature." How then does the recognition process develop? By being careful to "teach the thing before the name" as an original *Parents' Review* (September 1899) article put it. They'll learn the name when the item is present and they need a name for it. So we teach them the correct term like pollen or antennae instead of "sticky-up-thing." Miss Pennethorne says we want the children to have "awe, wonder, reverence and [to see] our own insignificance" (original *P.R.* September 1899) and to see the Creator in the created.

Nature Walks: One afternoon a week we will take the children out for a nature walk. These are not instructive walks because we want them to observe with very little direction from us. One reason is that science should be studied in an ordered sequence, which is not possible with the randomness you will encounter out walking. The parent may be asked questions, and it is permissible to answer; that's why it is recommended we work on our nature knowledge somewhat. There is nothing wrong with not knowing and looking it up at home in a field guide. You can invite a naturalist to come with you provided you can locate one and they agree to follow the C. Mason method to some degree. I have used private property for these walks, with permission, and often the owner enjoys supplying a little information about the plant life or animal life of their area. You should attempt to visit the same area quarterly to note how the seasons have altered the life.

A good time of year to begin observing trees, according to Edward M. Tuttle, is in the winter when the trees are bare. He wrote an in-depth article for the original *Parents' Review* on how to study trees which was reprinted in Volume 2 (Winter 1992-1993) of the current *P. R.* that you may order if you wish to read it. This approach could be used on trees in your yard as well as trees in the forest, I believe. You can sketch the tree, noting the branches and the bark. Mr. Tuttle also wisely suggests we observe what birds and insects live in the trees we are visiting. He suggests we find out what purpose trees are used for, such as syrup, nuts, or the wood.

I love this next idea of Mr. Tuttle's, and I can't wait to do this. Get sample pieces of woods in lengthwise and crosswise cuts and compare the natural state of it to the "finished" state of being oiled and polished. You could try collecting samples from your local lumberyard. One source I've found for mail-order wood samples is a company called Woodcraft. They offer a Wood Identification Kit that includes fifty 4"x9" samples at $19.99. It comes with a list of species, botanical names, and country of origin. You can write for their catalog at 210 Wood County Industrial Park, P. O. Box 1686, Parkersburg, WV 26102-1686 or call them at 1-800-535-4482. They have retail outlets in various major cities throughout the country, which you'll find listed in the catalog.

What happens with all this knowledge the children are getting as they are out? They are recording it in their **nature notebooks**—also known as a nature diary. The only information recorded in these books is the firsthand observation the child has done. The information for these does not come from teaching. The notebooks are voluntary and are never made mandatory. We do not correct or look for spelling errors or any of that. Rather, if you have a reluctant child, the more they can trust that their book will not be looked at or compared with others, the more willing they may become to attempt one. They are begun as soon as the child is old enough to write or draw. They often become a lifetime hobby as they are very enjoyable. All the Charlotte Mason mothers I know are keeping them because they like it.

Do not let a lack of artistic talent keep you from it. I could only draw stick people and the same fat, blobby cats someone showed me to draw when I was young. I, like so many others, am amazed that I have artistic ability of any kind. The reason we are succeeding at drawing is, we are **really** looking at what we draw. Place the specimen on a white background and draw what you see to size. Do not draw any backgrounds. You may take your notebooks out with you and sketch and/or bring home samples to draw later.

To have a successful notebook, provide a large variety of specimens. It will look very dull if all you ever draw is leaves. All the parent has to do is give the opportunity to observe nature and supply the child with the best artistic equipment available. I like the economical aspects of the C. Mason method, but this is one area to splurge a little in. Charlotte does not want children to fail because they have bad equipment. For the notebook, I buy sketch pads with spiral binding so that they open flat. It also states on the cover that they are usable outdoors. We switched to sketch pencils instead of ordinary pencils because I took Charlotte's advice on this, and she was right, it makes a big difference. They need the best colored pencils and watercolors.

They can label the drawings with both the English and Latin name. You may assist them in locating a name if they need help. They can note the location where they found the entry. An occasional poem pertaining to nature is a good idea. Some nature notebooks include a lot of notations of what the temperature is or the weather. Lists of animals and birds seen are good, too (they are hard to sketch since they insist on moving so much). Life cycles and developing buds on tree limbs are also favorite choices. They can describe an ant hill they saw and what the ants appeared to be doing. The rising and setting times of the sun can be noted. Some families also record the science experiments they do in their notebooks.

Some other science ideas are pressing and mounting flowers on cardboard. Write their names and where and when you found them. I recently saw a photo-album used to store pressed flowers. Having a field guide to identify flowers and flowering trees is very helpful. A calendar devoted to nature observation could be kept with simple entries on when the leaves first fell or the fruit tree in your yard first ripened for the year. Children should know the leaves of their neighborhood. They should be noticing some leaves are heart shaped, some are divided, and some fall off in the winter. With time they should be able to distinguish between petal, sepal, and other flower parts. They should see on their own that some creatures have backbones and some do not. Give them a pocket compass and possibly a microscope. We like using the magnifying glass better. Buy the best one you can afford and check it at the store—they seem to vary in how they focus. Charlotte says to teach children to notice winds and tell them the wind is named by what direction it comes from; for example, yourself being an American because you are born in America—you do not become a Canadian when you go to Canada. Have them walk a distance and then measure how far they've walked.

City children can try to feed and observe city birds such as sparrows. They can place a caterpillar in a box with a netting over it and watch it spin. Keeping an ant farm is suggested, and we had a good one this past winter. Have them go to the pond, gather some frogs' eggs, and place them in a large glass jar. After the tadpoles begin to form legs, take them back and release them at the pond. It was suggested children keep silkworms but I have no personal experience with that. The point is, even in the city, they should get their knowledge of nature first hand and get into the habit of being in touch with nature. Incidentally, Charlotte would not teach the young children to pull flowers apart in the name of botany or destroy life.

Charlotte had some real boldness when she said in *A Philosophy of Education* (Vol. 6, pg. 218) "we should probably be more scientific as a people if we **scrapped** all the **textbooks**." As I said previously, you can use the textbooks you have on hand as outlines or references. You can use narration with textbooks; however, living books are a better choice. Scientific living books are challenging to find. You want a literary quality to them, and above all you want them interesting. A biography of a scientist's life would be a good start. When you find a good book like I'm attempting to describe, by all means tell your friends and your support group. We can all use as much help with this as possible. The PNEU schools went in an orderly sequence so they would select books on natural history, botany, architecture, astronomy, and other branches of science and take each subject term by term. (A term was sixty school days.) Keep in mind you only want to get a little help from books since you do not want all your knowledge from books alone. The parent is encouraged to research so he/she is able to answer questions.

CHARLOTTE'S RECOMMENDATIONS

The Sciences—Edward Singleton Holden (1846 to 1914). It is out of print but check for an interlibrary loan. The Seattle (Washington) Public Library might have it. It may also be titled *Real things in Nature* (1914) available at the University of Washington.

Life and Her Children—Arabella Buckley (1840-1929)

Madam How and Lady Why—Charles Kingsley. The 1911 edition is at Washington State University, and the 1920 edition is at the University of Montana.

Parables From Nature—Mrs. Alfred Gatty (Margaret Scott Gatty). The 1914 edition is at the University of Montana, Whitman College in Washington State, Garland at Washington State University, and the Anchorage (Alaska) Library.

Picciola

Scientific Dialogues—Joyce

MY LIST

Handbook of Nature Study—Comstock

Wild Animals I Have Known—Seton

The Christian Liberty Nature Readers—Christian Liberty Press

Birds do the Strangest Things—Hornblow

The Country Diary of an Edwardian Lady—Edith Holden

Drawn From New England—Bethany Tudor

Miss Hickory—Bailey

Louis Pasteur (a biography)—Sower Series; Mott Media

Various field guides

I obtained most of these based on Karen Andreola's recommendations and am quite pleased with them. Check with Great Christian Books for availability.

MATH

Charlotte Mason has an interesting viewpoint on math. She noticed it is easy material to test a person on—every problem is either right or it is wrong. This is why she feels undue importance has been placed on math. She wants people to study math for its "own sake and not as they [mathematics] make for general intelligence and grasp of mind." She feels that a mathematician who doesn't know history is "sparsely educated at best." While approving of math genius she also wonders why should a person's "success in life depend upon drudgery in mathematics" and his or her possible exclusion from a university.

Having said that, Charlotte does feel that math is necessary, that it takes the **entire attention**, and that we are as invigorated by regular spells of hard exercise in it as we are with bodily exercise. To achieve full attention, we rely on short lessons. Present one difficulty at a time to the child's mind. We need to give them time to think without boring them. Remember in C. Mason's method we do not cram. The Hon. Mrs. E. L. Franklin tells us that slow progress with the math rules is our goal, and she assures us that the child will not fall behind.

Parents have incorporated narration in math. In other words ask them to tell you all they know about a concept they have studied. This could be done after studying one particular concept for a period of time or even used daily after each lesson.

HOW TO: Teach the children the concrete before the abstract no matter how old they are. When they are young always have them use "counters." I have been using dried beans for years as they are inexpensive and do not spoil. Charlotte prefers beans, buttons, and dominoes over cubes. Give the children story problems and let them use their beans to solve it. When they can add or subtract up to twenty, introduce multiplication and division using beans. They will see right away that multiplication is the same as addition only faster. Let them use "counters" all they want. On their own they will begin working with imaginary beans as their first step to abstract numbers. Mary Everest Boole's advice in an original *Parents' Review* (September 1893) was that "no child should use a multiplication table until he has made one" and that it may take months to complete. She advised we let the child learn through experience the faster and easier ways to do any type of math.

Daily mental effort, one step at a time, will give the child the habit of concentration. Encourage clear thinking and rapid, careful execution. Let them learn from experience that math is exact by having them see wrong is wrong. Let their wrong answer remain wrong. In my zeal to get my money's worth from every workbook, I formerly had my children re-do each incorrect problem. Charlotte wants them to try to get the next one right, to **have hope**.

When teaching money, she wants them to learn with real money. I've done that but I also have a flannel set of toys, paper money, and coins we enjoy using. When learning weights and measures, she wants them to weigh and measure. She suggests they weigh out four ounce bags of sand or rice as an example. Have them guess the weight of an object, such as a book, and then weigh it. The time to introduce fractions, she says, is while they are learning measurements. Supply them with a yard stick and have them measure objects around them. Another tip I found helpful was when teaching place values to children, refer to it as carry the two "tens" rather than simply carry the two.

Miss Pennethorne's original *Parents' Review* (September 1899) article suggests we teach some math concepts by sight. Most of us probably have a multiplication table posted on the wall we could have the child drill. She also suggests putting concepts on the board to get a mental photograph, for example:

$$6=5+1 \quad 6=3+3 \quad 6=2+2+2$$
$$6=8-2 \quad 6=3\text{x}2 \quad 6=2\text{x}3$$
$$6\div3=2 \quad 6\div2=3$$

In conclusion, you could use any curriculum you may already have on hand; it can be adapted to these methods. For example, most math books are going to be long-lesson oriented. We set our timer for fifteen minutes, stop when it rings, and resume right there the next day. The time allotted for math in junior and senior high increases to thirty minutes if done 6 days a week. (See Appendix)

Do not overlook teaching the concrete before the abstract even when approaching algebra and geometry. This will avoid "when will we ever need this???" whining. There is a useful book Garlic Press has made available from their Straight Ahead math series called *Applying Algebra*. Each lesson addresses how a certain profession would use a certain formula. If you can't find it locally write to The Home School Books and Supplies at 104 S. West Ave., Arlington, WA 98223 or call 1-800-788-1221.

ART APPRECIATION

Charlotte Mason is very consistent. In this subject, as in previous ones, we are **not** going to be the middleman. We are going to allow them direct contact with the best art. Therefore, the child will learn about pictures from the pictures themselves not from lectures or books about schools of art. The ideal way is to obtain six reproductions (of at least 8"x11" proportions) of one artist's work. The PNEU schools spent sixty school days on these six works, and at the end of the term they asked the child which was their favorite from the collection.

This was begun at six years old, and they spent about ten minutes a week studying art. Look for prints at museum gift shops, antique stores, and frame shops. If you have difficulty finding individual prints at a decent price then borrow a book from the library on one artist at a time. Adapt the book to the method by narrowing to six or so pieces to study. If you're like me, you may want to place self-stick notepad sheets over any objectionable scenes or body parts. This is one reason I like to choose individual prints—it's up to my personal discretion what to select and helps eliminate a constant patrolling over the art book from inappropriate peeking. If you purchase a book, you are free, of course, to remove an entire page. I collect art print catalogs as often as possible because they are inexpensive and educational. With these, a sticker or black marker can reduce objectionable content.

HOW TO: Charlotte writes of art study in *Home Education* (Vol. 1), *School Education* (Vol. 3), and *A Philosophy of Education* (Vol. 6). The method is rather easy and very effective. Have the child **really** look at the picture, take in every detail, and give him as much time as he needs. If I'm showing the print to more than one child, I give each one an individual turn of seeing it up close. Now, take away the print and look at it yourself, so that they cannot see it anymore. Have them describe what they saw from memory starting with the youngest child present. This will challenge the older ones to seek out detail the younger ones may overlook. From the first try, I was overwhelmed with the accuracy of my children's descriptions. Beyond description you may ask them what time of day it is in the picture, if there is a story behind it, whether they liked it, or thought it was gloomy. Aside from this intense observing, we are told to decorate our school rooms with reproductions of the masters.

This will lead to visiting museums and galleries as you are able. It is important for them to see the size of the actual work. You can explain to them all you want, but they need to see the real thing. This will also lead them to try art work for themselves, which, of course, you do encourage. Later, when they are much older, some study of the technicalities of composition, shading, and styles may be done.

ART THE CHILDREN DO

The children are encouraged to illustrate favorite passages that come along in their reading. I once illustrated the entire book of Revelation and learned firsthand what a powerful learning tool this could be. However, as with nature notebooks, true progress in ability comes from looking at what you are going to draw. Supply them with quality equipment as mentioned in the nature notebook section of Science. They can also do clay modeling and various other crafts, which is covered in the section on Free-Time Handicrafts.

MUSIC APPRECIATION

Charlotte wants us to play the greatest music for our children. Once again, we can achieve this goal at no cost, if we choose to. I am certain most major cities have a classical music station available. With the selections usually being long in duration, it can be the most pleasant radio listening. We turn the volume down to screen out the commercials. The other economical solution is to borrow classical music from the library and as you develop favorites purchase just those. It also seems as though some of the best bargains at the music stores are on classical music.

If you need some orientation on what a concerto is or any information like this, you may want a copy of *Music of the Great Composers* by Patrick Kavanaugh (formerly published as *A Taste for the Classics*). This book is easy and enjoyable. Everyone likes his other book, *The Spiritual Lives of Great Composers*, which contains short biographies of many composers in chronological order of their life spans. This is a good book for narrations. Both of these are available through Great Christian Books and Christian Supply.

You are free to approach this subject any way that suits your family. You could organize your selections around one composer at a time or simply play good music in the background. If you want your children to accept this style of music, it's easier to start young; but if your children are older, it is still not too late. I have one teenage child who was somewhat reluctant at first, but she now has developed a taste for classical. You can combine history and music study together by either being very observant while reading your history or by looking up the musical development of an era in a book such as *The Timetables of History* by Bernard Grun.

MUSICAL TRAINING FOR CHILDREN

Charlotte's first and foremost concern here was that children learn from an artist and not from what she referred to as ill-qualified, mechanical music teachers. Another concern was that they start early in life, and the PNEU strongly suggested something known as the Curwen method, named after Mrs. Spencer Curwen. Mrs. Curwen insisted the piano is the best first instrument. R. A. Pennethorne's article from the original *Parents' Review* (September 1899) summarizes the Curwen method to be "read by sight, write from ear, make his own scales, and transpose simple tunes, before he attempts to play" much past the beginning level. Compared to this, we are very relaxed at our house. We make available the recorder, a piano, and some guitars. I teach the children to read music, but they have not yet participated in any formal lessons. Each family can choose what instruments you want to expose your children to and how far you wish to take their instruction.

FREE-TIME HANDICRAFTS

The Charlotte Mason method is known for giving children free time in the afternoons and evenings. There is no structured school work scheduled at anytime other than the mornings. She wants the children to have time to be children without the adults always structuring their time. However, she cautions us in this area by pointing out that parents home school their children to save them from the corruption of public school only to turn around and possibly give them **too much** leisure time. This, in her opinion, will allow sin to creep into their lives. She tells us parents that the child needs absorbing, interesting work and that his mind should be "continually and wholesomely occupied." To accomplish this, we strive to teach them handicrafts in a slow and careful way. We don't give them **futile work**. We don't want sloppy work. We do not have to hurry the handicrafts.

Some of the upcoming suggestions may be things we don't know how to teach. Recently, two books have come to my attention, *The American Boy's Handy Book* and *The American Girl's Handy Book*, by the Beards. I have not personally spent time with these books but at first glance they looked very good. Lifetime Books has carried them and can be ordered by writing to 3900

Chalet Suzanne Dr., Lake Wales, FL 33853-7763. Or call 1-800-377-0390 for orders and 941-676-6311 for questions. These books are also available through Home School Supply House at P. O. Box 2000, 280 W. Center St., Beaver, UT 84713. The Whole Heart Catalog no longer carries these books but does have a section on family fun and games, and they carry many of the Charlotte Mason resources. You may to write to them at P. O. Box 228, Route 1 Box 617A, Walnut Springs, TX 76690 or call 817-797-2142. Another book to watch for or borrow from the library is *Victorian Family Celebrations*, also known as *Mrs. Sharp's Traditions*, by Sarah Ban Breathnach. I could not rave enough about this book. It's done month by month to equip you to turn to the appropriate time of year and then supplies you with many inspiring ideas of things to do with and for your family. (Personally, I ignore the Halloween section.)

When the children are six and a half to seven and a half, the Hon. Mrs. E. L. Franklin says to supply them with sand to play with and water for floating. She also suggests they play with stone, bricks, paper, and balls, and that these are superior to educational toys that break. Charlotte writes that when the child is under nine we have them doing chair-caning, basket work, rugs, carving in cork, stitching, and knitting for a few examples. Mrs. Franklin seconds the chair-caning and knitting and adds painting, clay modeling, wood carving, and bent iron work.

Many of the contributors suggested gardening as a useful activity. Margaret Donovan wrote an article on this which has been reprinted in the current *Parents' Review*; back order Vol. 1 (Winter 1991) if you wish to read it. She had many helpful suggestions, such as keeping the children's garden a peaceful sanctuary where they can leave their worries behind when they enter it. She would also like them to cook and eat what they grow. We are not to supervise the planning too much but allow them to learn from experience how a designed garden looks compared to a random one. There is a cute idea of keeping an indoor garden in the winter time by planting shallow rooting plants in a tray. Add some garden paths by breaking up some rocks for gravel. Use some moss and water frequently.

PHYSICAL EXERCISE

Bodily training was very important to Charlotte and the other PNEU participants, and she writes about it in *Home Education* pages 80–85. Charlotte mentions badminton and skipping rope as good outdoor activities. Calisthenics is another often-mentioned subject in Charlotte Mason material. She says to "give the child pleasure in light and easy motion...dancing, drill, calisthenics, some sort of judicious physical exercise, should [be] part of every day's routine." (*Home Ed.* p. 132) The physical activities seemed to revolve around singular sports more than large group sports.

Miss Pennethorne warns us to keep the physical exercise noncompetive reminding us that "we don't train 'prize pigs,' we educate children."

BIBLE

In Charlotte's book *School Education* (Vol. 3) she writes, "Perhaps, there has been some falling off both in national intelligence and character since the Bible has been practically deposed for the miscellaneous 'reader'." Obviously, as we are living nearly one hundred years later, we have seen the results of removing the Bible from public schools entirely. Naturally, as Christian home schooling families, we are teaching the Bible to our children. We *are* using the Bible, right? Everywhere I researched how Charlotte Mason students were taught the Bible, one thing was repeated time and time again—**use just the Bible.** This chapter could have consisted of only that sentence. I could not agree more. There are many curriculums available and many watered down little books claiming to be your solution to teaching this subject. There is great power in the actual Word of God, and no other book compares with the book our Creator authored. Charlotte was also opposed to paraphrases being read to children. She thought the child would retain through life those Bible scenes and even the words. She wanted their minds and imaginations to be stored with Scriptures. In *Home Education* (Vol. 1), she wrote, "they will see that the world is a stage whereon the goodness of God is continually striving with the willfulness of man; that some heroic men take sides with God; and that others, foolish and headstrong, oppose themselves to Him."

Charlotte wants the child to know that their Bible lessons are their most important. Rev. Henry Seeley wrote an article for the original *Parents' Review* (January 1895), where he stressed this point also. Communicate to them that the Bible is different than other books and that it is not just another subject. I know we already know this, but I'm hoping that we, in our zeal and freedom to teach God's truths, are not neglecting to keep this foremost in our children's minds. Rev. Seeley also wrote to be careful not to give the student a dislike for the Bible. Charlotte called it "undue rubbing-in of the Bible." Both the Reverend and Charlotte wanted only accurate Bible art to be shown to the children. He cautions us to watch our hymns as well, to be certain they are not contrary to Bible teaching. Another concern he had for us was not to make them read the Bible as a punishment.

Rev. Seeley suggests we pray before reading our Bibles, and the students should learn the names of the Bible books in order. Some other advice he had was to learn the groupings such as historical, prophetical, and the gospels. Always use scriptural terms when teaching doctrine. You could conduct Bible drills (what we call sword drills), having the children see who can find a verse, book, or names in the Bible first.

As with any other subject, use narration. They may write and illustrate their narrations and keep them in a folder, or perhaps one special book could hold all their Bible narrations. When they are six to eight years old,

Charlotte wants us to read to them from the Old Testament and New Testament. This grounds the New Testament teaching on the Old Testament. The object, she writes in *A Philosophy of Education* (Vol. 6), is to give "such a full and gradual picture of the O. T. History that they unconsciously perceive for themselves a panoramic view of the history of mankind..."

Following, is the sequence suggested by Charlotte Mason:

AGE

6 to 8	Read to them both O.T. and N.T. concentrating on the Gospels and Acts
By 9	Read to themselves simple O.T. passages and two of the Gospels
By 12	They have covered **all** the O.T. and have concentrated on the Epistles and Revelation
12 to 15	Read to themselves **all** the O.T.
15 to 18	Read commentaries*

*My personal opinion differs on this point. My emphasis is to teach and equip them at this age to handle the Word of God accurately. They are trained to do inductive study with ample time to do original language word studies.

HISTORY

Charlotte did not think enough history was being taught in the schools in her day. Apparently, they were fond of giving sketchy outlines of history, blaming a lack of time to do the job properly. She solves this problem by using narration and claims this will quadruple our time enabling us to "get through a surprising amount of history in a thorough way." (Vol. 6, p. 171)

Charlotte's students were taught history in chronological order. They did not want to bore the children so they were very particular to choose interesting books. They used literature, plays, novels, essays, biographies, poetry, architecture, and paintings of the period. The idea is to read someone's firsthand account who saw what happened whenever possible. Her students were allowed to spend time "pleasantly" with one time period in the life of maybe even one man. She believes if you spent a whole year with one man you would really be learning about a whole nation and the whole time period he lived in. Make sure the children are aware of what the ordinary people's conditions were and what the "great" people were doing. I find the *Timetables of History* to be a helpful beginning for this. The point is, she thinks it would be better to know as much as they can about even one short period than to know the outlines of history.

HOW TO: The six year olds under Charlotte's direction were read about forty pages per term (sixty days), from a well-written, well-illustrated large book. They did not use books written down to the child's level. They did not choose books full of little summaries. They would amplify this with short biographies of the people involved with the time period they were studying. She also wanted them to visit the monuments at this age, and if that were not possible then look at pictures of them in books. She said this built "sane and serviceable patriotism."

From nine to twelve years old they illustrated their history lesson when they were in a chapter that dealt with the social life of a period. At this age she wanted them to study the history of countries other than their own to avoid an "arrogant habit of mind." (I agree with this concept, and I am concerned about the preoccupation with United States history. To prove my point, when you go to the home school curriculum exhibits, do you see any living books to choose from covering Canada or any South American country?) At this age they were also careful to compare what was occurring in other countries at the same time period they were studying.

At twelve to fourteen, her children (who were living in Europe) studied India. By this age they knew English and French history. They also covered Greek and Roman history by using biographies. *Plutarch's Lives* was very highly thought of by the PNEU.

From fifteen to eighteen years old they read literature and concentrated on Greek and Roman history thoroughly. They liked to have them illustrating at this age, scenes from books like *Plutarch's Lives,* for example. This is a form of narration. What a child can visualize or imagine enough to illustrate, they know.

Projects would include having young children act out scenes from their history with their dolls, or if they are older have them paint some scenery and act it out.

They can make **history charts**. Using a large sheet of paper, make one hundred squares on it, ten spaces by ten spaces. This is a century and each square is a year. Invent a symbol for each major event, like a war. If your "war" is a picture of a gun, for example, then for each year there was a war, you would draw a gun in that year. The result should be a century at a glance. I think this could be a very enjoyable and absorbing project, requiring much research. I suppose this could be attempted on a computer, using some built-in graphics.

They can make a **time line**, we are told, on a sheet of paper. Make columns with the first century in the middle. Each column represents a century. All you have room for is a small notation and you do not have to worry about the exact dates, just the order of events.

Now, the famous **book of the centuries**. No doubt, you have seen these available to purchase. No offense intended to the manufacturer of this product, but they are not exactly giving this away. If you already own one, good—use it. If you have not yet bought one, don't. The exact details of how to make your own were written in an original *Parents' Review* that was reprinted in the current *Parents' Review*, Volume 2 (Fall 1992). That's right, this is not a new invention; the PNEU schools were using them. I decided not to follow the very detailed instructions provided in this article. Instead, I bought a large, three-ring binder and plenty of sketch paper. I had to punch holes in the paper so I could have sketchable paper. You could buy blank paper with the holes already punched if you wanted to. The "right" way to do this is to provide one blank and one lined sheet of paper per century. I even left out the lined paper in mine. I'm also really bending the rules by not constricting the child to only one page per century. Some centuries have a lot of crucial events take place during them, and I want the child to cover as many of these as he or she chooses to.

The purpose of the book is to have a place to make notations or illustrations of a historical event they have studied. Even though I've allowed more than one sheet, we still enforce the brief notation rule. Every book you read or museum you visit should provide a quick notation. This is a running time line for them. Charlotte believes children have very capable minds and that they make connections all the time mentally (which is why our family does not make a big issue of chronological order); the book of the centuries provides a place to record these connections. This book should last your children until they are eighteen years old or older, so we are warned by G. M. Bernau in the *P. R.* article to leave the more difficult subject matter until they are old enough to deal with it well. Some suggestions given are sketching events, museum artifacts, costumes, ships, weapons, or musical instruments. It is not all sketching by any means; they can simply write a quick name and life span of an author or composer. They can use the occasional photograph (or photocopy) or a newspaper clipping as well. They also included ten blank pages in the back for map work. One more really good idea from the article concerning this is keeping a **family** book of the centuries. Each family member could make contributions to it.

CHARLOTTE'S RECOMMENDATIONS

Ecclesiastical History of England—Bede

Plutarch's Lives—Plutarch

Chronicles of the Crusades—Devizes & deVinsany

Alton Locke—Kingsley

Silas Marner—George Eliot

Prisoners of the Tower—Brooke Hunt

Westward Ho—Kingsley

Old Stories from British History—York Powell

Quentin Druward—Sir Walter Scott

Sketches from British History—York Powell

The Talisman—Sir Walter Scott

Tales from St. Paul's—Mrs. Frewen Lord

Julius Caesar

Tales from Westminster Abbey—Mrs. Frewen Lord

A History of England—H. O. Arnold Forster

Shorter History of England—Green

History of the British Kings—Geoffrey

MY LIST

The History of the World—Kingfisher

The Timetables of History—Grun

Plutarch's Lives—Plutarch

Conversations with Pioneer Women—Lockley

Women's Diaries of the Westward Journey—Schlissel

The Tragedy of Leschi—Meeker

Going to School in 1776—Loeper

If You Were There in 1776*—Brenner

What Jane Austen Ate & Charles Dickens Knew—Pool

The Sower Series biographies—Mott Media

If You Grew Up with...—Scholastic

Oregon Trail, Lewis and Clark, etc. published as *The Story Behind the Scenery*

Albert Schweitzer, Elizabeth the First, etc.—A Rookie Biography (written to the child's level for certain, but make for good reading material for young readers)

*Not the same as the "If You Grew Up With..." series

GEOGRAPHY

According to Charlotte, children want the same geographical information as adults want. And we adults do not want to be bored. If we wanted to know about a place we would want to read an interesting travel book. She tells us we would skip the dry parts, and we most likely would not memorize the heights of all the mountains or the import/export statistics. They used travel guides in the PNEU schools because they have literary language. They read them to the children and the children narrated. Again, they cannot tell what they have not seen in their imaginations. Charlotte does not think pictures are necessary. However, I do use books containing them in our school as there are many gifted photographers in our day and the technology has greatly improved. *Sante Fe Trail—The Story Behind the Scenery* is an example of beautiful geographical pictures. Miss Pennethorne says the point is to go for ideas; not to teach **all** about Africa, for example. They want the child to be inspired enough to want to visit the area they've read about. Perhaps they even used Charlotte Mason's geography books she authored.

HOW TO: When the children are six to nine years old, read to them well-chosen travel books. Note the manners and any descriptions of the people living there.

Try both hot and cold climates. Study a region that will educate them regarding the sea. Teach the child of this age the points of direction. Before they study maps, have them draw one of their room. Then learn latitude and longitude. Before they discuss rivers, let them look at a stream. Before studying lakes, go out and see a pond.

When they are older, her students gave a lot of attention to map work. Before they read a book, they would look up the location on the map. They became familiar with Europe before they studied the countries separately. They would check to see what other continents would lie within the same parallels as the one they were studying. When her students were in tenth to twelfth grades they kept up with the newspapers and learned about the regions currently making the news. Supply them with a good atlas at this age.

My children like to trace maps on tracing paper. If it comes out especially well we cover them with clear contact paper. We have the Pacific Puzzle Company puzzles—one of the United States and one of the world. These are made of beechwood so they last. They are also challenging because the empty area is not marked. You have to **know** where each country goes. The Pacific Puzzle Company can be contacted at P. O. Box 1001 Anacortes, WA 98221 or call 800-467-0242.

CITIZENSHIP AND MORALS

Charlotte suggests we use the Bible and *Plutarch's Lives* for this subject. Plutarch does not judge people as good or bad so the children are free to make their own judgment calls. You can read Plutarch to elementary school-aged children according to Charlotte, just censor out some passages. In *Philosophy of Education* (Vol. 6, p. 187) she says she wants the child to see life whole but they must be protected from "grossness and rudeness by means of the literary medium through which they are taught."

In Charlotte Mason's book *Ourselves* (Vol. 4, Book 2, pgs. 33–40) there is an interesting section using several examples from literature on moral behavior. Using Steerforth from *David Copperfield* among others she demonstrates how incorrect choices made, when faced with temptation, result in misery. This is another example of using books instead of censoring fictional material so they can learn from other's mistakes.

Charlotte's students read *Ourselves* when they

were older, and they were taught to keep watch over their thoughts and to keep their minds pure and decent.

THE FORMATION OF HABIT

An interesting place to get a feel of Charlotte Mason's definition of habit can be found in her book *Formation of Character* (Vol. 5, pgs. 6–8). She details for us a story of a father of two children feeding birds on the windowsill every morning at 7:55. The birds punctually gather at the sill every morning for one month. The children are not sure how the birds know what time it is. One day, no crumbs are put out on purpose so they can observe that the birds will still come punctually and regularly. They stayed as long as before and flew off without any sign of disappointment. Now they are coming just out of habit, which Charlotte defines as "a mere automatic or machine-like action with which conscious thought has nothing to do." The father then turns his attention to breaking the hereditary habit of barking in his dog. These stories were given to show "the automatic nature of the action once the habit is formed."

In Charlotte Mason's book *Home Education* (Vol. 1), you will find the longest and most comprehensive portion of material on habit. Pages 96 through 168 are must reading. To summarize, she saw the will of children as weak. Some examples are how they are given to be idle, tell fibs, and dawdle. The problem for the educator is to give the child control over his own nature. She teaches us that thoughts defile a man and thoughts purify a man. That we think as we are accustomed to think and we get into ruts. The outcome is that we do not deliberately intend to think these thoughts. She says the child is "immature of will, feeble in moral power, unused to the weapons of the spiritual warfare." (pg. 109)

Charlotte's belief is that habits of thought will govern the man, even his character. You will find her often likening habits in the human life to rails for the train. The same way it is easier for the train to stay on the rails than to leave them, so it is for the child to follow lines of habit carefully laid down than to run off these lines. It is the very serious responsibility of the parent to lay down these tracks. Habit is so powerful according to Charlotte that it will rule 99 in 100 of our thoughts and acts. This will happen whether you formed the habits or not. To quote her from page 111, "even in emergencies, in every sudden difficulty and temptation that requires an act of will, why, conduct is still apt to run on the lines of the familiar habit. The boy who has been accustomed to find both profit and pleasure in his books does not fall easily into idle ways because he is attracted by an idle schoolfellow. The girl who has been carefully trained to speak the exact truth simply does not think of a lie as a ready means of getting out of a scrape, coward as she may be."

Charlotte Mason believed habits involve physiological factors so we should teach dancing, swimming, and other physical things early in life. The same concept applies with stooping and indistinct utterance; these will not just go away later because the child knows better. He will not be able to habitually speak better because his body has formed. She believed even moral habits have an effect on physical tissues in the brain.

We could spend some time considering some of our constant repetition of thoughts we have and how habitual they are. Charlotte reminds us of how long a time a soldier takes to learn his drill and how automatic it becomes, such as when even a veteran responds when someone yells "attention." Bringing us to the point made on page 118, "the habits of the child produce the character of the man, because certain mental habitudes once set up, their nature is to go on for ever unless they should be displaced by other habits. Here is an end to the easy philosophy of, 'It doesn't matter,' 'Oh, he'll grow out of it,' 'He'll know better by-and-by,' 'He's so young, what can we expect?' and so on. Every day, every hour, the parents are either passively or actively forming those habits in their children upon which, more than upon anything else, future character and conduct depend."

HOW TO: Charlotte explains on page 119 of *Home Education* the process of overcoming a bad habit with a good habit, using dawdling as the example. The mother must know she is to devote herself to this for a few weeks "as steadily and untiringly as she would to the nursing of her child through measles." The mother should briefly point out the miseries that must arise from this fault and the duty of overcoming it. Then get the child's will on the side of right doing. Mom sees for weeks together the fault does not recur. The next time the child dawdles she sees her mother looking at her. "The pauses become fewer day by day, the efforts steadier, the immature young will is being strengthened, the habit of prompt action acquired. After that first talk, the mother would do well to refrain from one more word on the subject; the eye (expectant, not reproachful), and, where the child is far gone in a dream, the lightest possible touch, are the only effectual instruments. By-and-by, 'Do you think you can get ready in five minutes today without me?' 'Oh yes, mother.' 'Do not say "yes" unless you are quite sure.' 'I will try.' And she tries, and succeeds. **Now, the mother will be tempted to relax her efforts— to overlook a little dawdling because the dear child has been trying so hard."** Don't do it. Time and time again when Charlotte is outlining this procedure for us, whether it's the math lesson or closing the door, she puts emphasis on the follow through. The dangerous time is just before the habit is formed. Don't let it go "just this once." You need to be consistent and patient.

We are told to act as a friendly ally, to help the child with the decision to do the new habit. The habit becomes easy and natural. The mother should not think the child is making a big effort; he is doing it automatically. A good habit will take a few weeks, and we are to guard it incessantly, but not anxiously. Prompt action on the child's part should have the reward of absolute leisure time in which to do exactly as she pleases. If the child completes her math in 10 minutes instead of the allotted 20 then the natural consequence of 10 free minutes is the reward. We are also instructed to leave the children alone as a gardener leaves the plant to do most of the work on its own with only a little pruning and watering.

With the hope that you are not overwhelmed with the idea of this being too much work, I would like you to know that Charlotte Mason considered habit a delight in itself and the training in habits becomes a habit for the mother. It is one habit at a time we are working on, and we merely watch over the habits already formed. She assures us in *School Education* (Vol. 3) that when the habit is fully formed supervision will no longer be necessary. At first the child wants the support of constant supervision but we leave him to do the thing he ought of his own accord. Remember her famous habit quote, "The mother who takes pains to endow her children with good habits secures for herself smooth and easy days; while she who lets their habits take care of themselves has a weary life of endless friction with the children. All day she is crying out, 'Do this!' and they do it not; 'Do that!' and they do the other."

Next, I would like to help and encourage you to read the six-volume set yourself. If it is habit you are interested in, you will find it to be the most repeated word in the set. I will provide some page numbers for specific referencing by topic.

Home Education (Vol. 1)

P. 86 Habit of Attention

P. 124 Infant 'Habits'—Topics include: Cleanliness, order, neatness, regularity, punctuality, prompt and intelligent replies, physical exercise, good manners drilled by play acting, and speaking clearly.

P. 137 The Habit of Attention—Covers wandering attention, explains how to never allow the child to dawdle over a copy book or sum or day-dream. P. 141 also includes how to make the lessons attractive, how to vary them so that the power of the child's mind may rest after effort. Each lesson must be done, but you may take away the lesson being dawdled over and give him another lesson to do as unlike it as possible. Then he can return to the other lesson refreshed.

P. 142 Time-Table; Definite Work in a Given Time— Explains how to train children in habits of order and diligence "he learns that one time is not 'as good as another'; that there is no right time left for what is not done in its own time; and this knowledge alone does a great deal to secure the child's attention to his work." Short lessons are addressed to keep their attention. On P. 146 the habit of inattention is combated by never allowing the child to do school work into which he does not put his heart.

P. 147 Wholesome Home Treatment for Mooning—This suggests we have something pleasant ready for when the lesson is completed in time.

P. 149 Rapid Mental Effort—"Aim steadily at securing quickness of apprehension and execution, and that goes far towards getting it" instead of letting them plod.

P. 150 The Habit of Thinking

P. 151 The Habit of Imagining—Don't give them too much nonsènse reading.

P. 154 The Habit of Remembering—Not cramming, not short-term memory. "You want the child to remember? Then secure his whole attention..."

P. 159 The Habit of Perfect Execution—Starts out with the habit of turning out imperfect work. No work should be given to a child that he cannot execute perfectly. Let everything be done well. Have him point out an imperfection and persevere until he has produced his task.

P. 160 Some Moral Habits—Obedience—This is a gradual training in the habit of obedience and an enlisting of his will to a sense of right. We don't want tardy, unwilling, occasional obedience. The habit of obedience is more prompt, cheerful, and lasting. "Never give a command which she (mother) does not intend to see carried out to the full."

P. 164 Habit of Truthfulness

Parents and Children (Vol. 2)

P. 62 The Habits of School Life are Mechanical

P. 124 The Minor Moralities Become Matters of Habit— "Educate the child in right habits and the man's life will run in them, without the constant wear and tear of the moral effort of decision. Once, twice, three times in a day, he will still, no doubt, have to choose between the highest and the less high, the best and the less good course. But all the minor moralities of life may be made habitual to him. He has been brought up to be courteous, prompt, punctual, neat, considerate; and he practices these virtues without conscious effort."

P. 159 The Law for Us—'One Custom Overcometh Another'—"[Habit]...may be begun in a moment, formed in a month, confirmed in three months, become the character, the very man, in a year."

P. 173 Good Habits the Best Schoolmasters

P. 174 Always Telling—When you find yourself always telling them to do the same thing, you have not trained them in the habits you wish they would do. "The well-brought-up child has always been a child carefully trained in good habits."

P. 175 Practical Counsels—Nine specific steps to deal with a seriously bad habit.

P. 234 Life-History of a Habit—"Every act proceeds from a thought."

P. 237 Habits of Well-Brought-Up Persons—"Diligence, reverence, gentleness, truthfulness, promptness, neatness, courtesy."

School Education (Vol. 3)

P. 20 The Habit of Prompt Obedience

P. 104 Use of Habit in Physical Training

P. 107 Self-Discipline and Local Habits

P. 108 Alertness

P. 109 Quick Perception

P. 110 Stimulating Ideas—"A habit becomes morally binding in proportion to the inspiring power of the idea which underlies it."

P. 118 The Formation of Intellectual Habits—Examples: Attention, concentration, thoroughness, intellectual volition, accuracy, and reflection.

P. 135 The Habit of Sweet Thoughts

P. 136 Virtues in Which Children Should be Trained—Examples: Candour, fortitude, temperance, patience, meekness, courage, and generosity.

P. 140 The Habits of the Religious Life—Includes Habit of the Thought of God, The Habit of Reading the Bible, and The Habit of Praise.

Ourselves (Vol 4)

P. 45 Habit Goes Always Over the Same Ground—"A good servant and a bad master."

P. 172 The Habit of Finishing

P. 207 The Habit of Being of Use

P. 208 The Law of Habit

Philosophy of Education (Vol. 6)

P. 99 Education is a Discipline—"We have lost sight of the fact that habit is to life what rails are to transport cars. It follows that lines of habit must be laid down towards given ends and after careful survey, or the joltings and delays of life become insupportable. More, habit is inevitable. If we fail to ease life by laying down habits of right thinking and right acting, habits of wrong thinking and wrong acting fix themselves of their own accord."

APPENDIX

In this section I have included weekly schedules used by the Charlotte Mason schools. Also, you will find a weekly timetable showing how many hours were dedicated to the subjects per week. Remember, the C. Mason students attended school six days a week. I have included these as a guideline, not as a strict schedule to adhere to. My own schedule (for my current school year) has been included to show how we all can adapt the method to suit our needs. My schedule has some academics in the afternoon because that's when the younger children nap. I also had to allow time for driving my oldest daughter back and forth to her college classes. When all my children are older and not napping I will teach the academics during the morning hours only, as Charlotte advises us to.

You will see my daily routine does not vary as much as the C. M. one does. To keep it simplified for me, all the children do the same subject at the same time. Fridays will be less structured than the rest of the week, but if we happen to fall behind we will make up for it on that day.

We will have devotions between breakfast and 9:00 when we begin our school day with math. Additional

Bible readings will be conducted during the read-aloud time.

Please do not let these schedules be your focus. Any schedule that works for your circumstances is what you should be using. I change mine fairly often because I reprioritize according to the children's changing needs. The point is, you should not lose sight of Charlotte's philosophy of having a definite timetable posted where the children can see it. Knowing what they are going to do and how long they have to do it is one of the strategies of training them not to dawdle during school time.

CHARLOTTE MASON'S WEEKLY SCHEDULE FOR THE FIRST–THIRD GRADES

	M	T	W	TH	F	S
9:00- 9:20	Old Testament	New Testament	Writing	Old Testament	New Testament	Week's Work
9:20- 9:40	Printing	Drawing	Reading	Reading	Reading	Reading
9:40- 9:50	Repetition Poem	Repetition Parable	Continue Reading	Continue Reading	Repetition Hymn	Continue Reading
9:50-10:00	French	Picture Talk	French	French	Natural History	Object Lesson
10:00-10:20	Number	Handicrafts	Number	Handicrafts	Number	Number
10:20-10:35	Drill or Dancing	Sol-fa play	Drill or Dancing	French Song Play	Drill or Dancing	Sol-fa Play
10:35-10:50						
10:50-11:20	Reading	Number	Handicrafts	Writing and Brush-Drawing	Handicrafts	Writing and Brush-Drawing
11:20-11:30	Natural History	Reading	Geography	Number	Geography	Natural History

Taken from the original *Parents' Review*, December 1908

Charlotte Mason's Weekly Schedule for the Fourth–Sixth Grades

	M	T	W	TH	F	S
9:00- 9:20	Old Testament	New Testament	Natural History	Old Testament	New Testament	Week's Work
9:20- 9:50	Arithmetic	Arithmetic	English History	Arithmetic	Arithmetic	Arithmetic
9:50-10:20	Dictation	Natural History	Dictation	Grammar	Plutarch's Lives	Latin
10:20-10:50	Drill 10m. Play	German Song 10m. Play	Drill 10m. Play	French Song 10m. Play	Drill 10m. Play	Sol-fa 10m. Play
10:50-11:00	Repetition Poem	Repetition Bible	Repetition Bible	Repetition Poem	Dictation	Repetition Week's Work
11:00-11:20	Geography	English History	Geography	French History	Grammar	Nature Lore
11:20-12:00	French	Latin	French	Reading	German	French

Taken from the original *Parents' Review*, December 1908

CHARLOTTE MASON'S WEEKLY SCHEDULE FOR THE SEVENTH–EIGHTH GRADES

	M	T	W	TH	F	S
9:00– 9:20	Old Testament	New Testament	Natural History	Old Testament	New Testament	Physical Geography
9:20– 9:50	Arithmetic	German	Arithmetic	English Grammar	Euclid	Arithmetic
9:50–10:20	Dictation	Composition	Dictation	Reading	Greek or Roman Lives	Latin
10:20–10:50	Drill 10m. Play	German Song 10m. Play	Drill 10m. Play	French Song 10m. Play	Drill 10m. Play	Sol-fa 10m. Play
10:50–11:00	Repetition Poem	Repetition Bible (O.T.)	Repetition Euclid	Repetition Poem	Repetition Bible (N.T.)	Repetition Week's Work
11:00–11:20	Geography	English History	Latin	English History	English Grammar	Botany
11:20–11:30	Arithmetic (Mental)	Arithmetic (Mental)	Map Questions	Arithmetic (Mental)	Writing	Euclid
11:30–12:15	French	Latin	Italian	French	German	Italian
12:15– 1:00	Botany	Geology	French History	Physiology	Geography	English Grammar

Taken from the original *Parents' Review*, December 1908

CHARLOTTE MASON'S WEEKLY SCHEDULE FOR THE NINTH GRADE

	M	T	W	TH	F	S
9:00- 9:30	Old Testament	New Testament	Latin	Old Testament	New Testament	Physical Geography
9:30-10:00	Arithmetic	Euclid	French	Arithmetic	Euclid	Algebra
10:00-10:40	Geology	Composition	Literature	Astronomy	Every-day Morals	Latin
10:40-11:00	Drill Singing	Drill Singing	Drill Singing	Drill Singing	Drill Singing	Drill Singing
11:00-11:45	Literature	English History	Geography	English History	Grammar	Botany
11:45-12:15	Botany	Algebra	European History	Every-day Morals	Geography	Grammar
12:15- 1:00	French	German	Italian	French	German	Italian

Taken from the original *Parents' Review*, December 1908

My Weekly Schedule

	M	T	W	TH	F
9:00- 9:20	Math	Math	Math	Math	
9:20- 9:40	Handwriting	Handwriting	Handwriting	Handwriting	
9:40-10:00	History	History	History	History	
10:00-10:50	Read aloud-Literature	Read aloud-Literature	Read aloud-Literature	Read aloud-Literature	
10:50	Drive to college	Drive to college	Drive to college	Drive to college	Drive to college
11:15-12:00	Lunch	Lunch	Lunch	Lunch	Lunch
12:00	Drill	Drill	Drill	Drill	College pick up
12:20-12:40	Science	Science	Science	Science	P.E. Social
12:40-1:00	Simply Grammar	Simply Grammar	Simply Grammar	Simply Grammar	P.E. Social
1:00-1:20	Latin	Music	Art Appr.	Poetry	P.E.
1:20-2:00	Map work	Children read aloud	Children read aloud	Children read aloud	P.E.

Charlotte Mason's Weekly Timetable

Grades One–Three (Periods 10-20 min.)

English	6 hrs. 20 min.
Arithmetic	1 hr. 50 min.
Science	1 hr. 10 min.
French	40 min.
Handicrafts	2 hrs.
Drill	3 hrs.
Total	15 hrs.

Grades Four–Six (Periods 20-30 min.)

English, 4th	7 hrs. 20 min.
5th & 6th	8 hrs. 50 min.
Mathematics	2 hrs. 30 min.
Science	2 hrs. 10 min.
Languages, 4th	1 hr. 30 min.
5th & 6th	3 hrs.
Drill, etc.	3 hrs.
Total, 4th	17 hrs.
5 & 6th	18 hrs. 30 min.

CHARLOTTE MASON'S WEEKLY TIMETABLE

GRADES SEVEN–NINE (PERIODS 20–45 MIN.)

English	8 hrs. 25 min.
Mathematics	3 hrs.
Science	3 hrs. 20 min
Languages	3 hrs. 45 min.
Drill, etc.	3 hrs.
Total	21 hrs. 30 min.

GRADES TEN–TWELVE (PERIODS 30-40 MINS.)

English; including History, Grammar, Literature, Economics, etc.	8 hrs. 10 min.
Mathematics	3 hrs.
Science	4 hrs. 10 min.
Languages	6 hrs. 10 min.
Drill	2 hrs. 30 min.
Total	24 hrs.

Taken from *A Liberal Education for All*, by Charlotte Mason